*PAUSE,

*BREATHE,

BE

A KID'S 30-DAY GUIDE TO
PEACE AND PRESENCE

BY MEGAN BORGERT-SPANIOL
AND LAUREN KUKLA
ILLUSTRATED BY
ARUNA RANGARAJAN

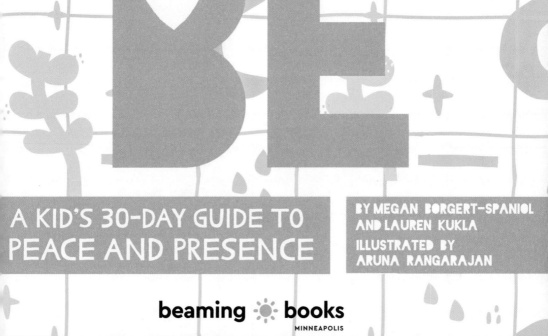

beaming books
MINNEAPOLIS

Photo Credits:
Cover: Bibadash/Shutterstock Images
Interior: Bibadash/Shutterstock Images, pp. 4, 5, 7, 8, 9, 10, 12, 16, 20, 22, 25, 26, 28, 32, 33, 36, 40, 44, 53, 54, 58, 62, 70, 74, 75, 76, 77, 80, 84, 88, 92, 99, 100, 106, 110, 114, 118, 122, 134, 138, 142, 144; Chris.Tea/Shutterstock Images, p. 34; Farid Huseynov/Shutterstock Images, p. 38; Nicetoseeya/Shutterstock Images, p. 48; Olga Strel/Shutterstock Images, p. 48; MURRIRA/Shutterstock Images, p. 66; Mary Long/Shutterstock Images, p. 126

28 27 26 25 24 23 22   1 2 3 4 5 6 7 8

Print ISBN: 978-1-5064-6993-5
eBook ISBN: 978-1-5064-7014-6

Library of Congress Cataloging-in-Publication Data

Names: Borgert-Spaniol, Megan, 1989- author. | Kukla, Lauren, author. |
  Rangarajan, Aruna, illustrator.
Title: Pause, breathe, be : a kid's 30-day guide to peace and presence / by Megan
Borgert-Spaniol & Lauren Kukla ; illustrations by Aruna Rangarajan.
Description: Minneapolis, MN : Beaming Books, 2022. | Audience: Ages 9-13 |
  Summary: "Through daily mantras, exercises, fun quizzes, and activities,
  Pause, Breathe, and Be: A Kid's 30-Day Guide to Peace and Presence
  encourages kids to engage in mindfulness one day at a time while
  building self-esteem and reducing anxiety"-- Provided by publisher.
Identifiers: LCCN 2021045840 (print) | LCCN 2021045841 (ebook) | ISBN
  9781506469935 (Hardcover) | ISBN 9781506470146 (eBook)
Subjects: LCSH: Mindfulness (Psychology)--Juvenile literature. |
  Self-esteem in children--Juvenile literature | Peace--Juvenile literature.
Classification: LCC BF637.M56 B67 2022 (print) | LCC BF637.M56 (ebook) |
  DDC 158.1--dc23
LC record available at https://lccn.loc.gov/2021045840
LC ebook record available at https://lccn.loc.gov/2021045841

VN0004589; 9781506469935; AUG2022

Beaming Books
PO Box 1209
Minneapolis, MN 55440-1209
Beamingbooks.com

CONTENTS

INTRODUCTION

Within this book are thirty challenges divided into three sections.

PAUSE

The first section, Pause, focuses on finding peace and presence within yourself.

BREATHE

The Breathe section centers on cultivating these things in your surroundings.

BE

And the final section, Be, explores creating peace and presence in your relationships with other people.

Are you noticing a theme? Finding peace and presence is a lifelong journey taken one day at a time.

EACH CHALLENGE IN THIS BOOK
WILL GUIDE YOU THROUGH
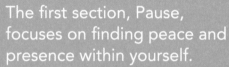 OF THIS JOURNEY.

You can work through the challenges in the order they're presented, or you can skip around based on what you need most on any given day. Maybe life has you feeling overwhelmed, so you start with a Breathe challenge. Maybe the next day your best friend is upset with you, so you flip to the Be challenges.

The way you move through this book is up to you, but we recommend aiming to complete every challenge at least once—even those that may not resonate with you right away. And give each challenge your all. Each one will aid you in learning to **Pause, Breathe,** and **Be.**

PAUSE.
Reconnect with yourself.

BREATHE.
Practice fully experiencing the here and now.

BE.
Reflect on and grow in the way you relate to others.

PAUSE

In today's world, we take part in so many activities. We juggle school, friends, family, sports practice, homework, and clubs. All the while, we manage a constant stream of news updates, social media feeds, shared videos, and text threads.

These activities can be fun, challenging, and entertaining. But we can sometimes lose ourselves in too many distractions. They often take time and focus away from getting to know our true selves, learning to enjoy time alone, and feeling a sense of peace.

The first ten challenges of this book invite you to pause and reconnect with yourself. This could mean gazing out a window and letting your buried thoughts surface. It might mean acknowledging emotions you've been trying to ignore. Or it might mean embracing the person you are right now, flaws and all.

CHALLENGES 1–10

When you pause, you can reflect on who you are. Knowing yourself will make you a more dynamic person. You'll be more able to roll with life's ups and downs, and you'll be more confident in your activities and interactions. Knowing yourself requires intention, but minimal time. As you work through the challenges ahead, you'll find that

EVERY DAY HOLDS SPARE MOMENTS TO PAUSE.

I WATCH AND WAIT FOR THOUGHTS TO RISE.

GAZE

TODAY, LOOK OUT THE WINDOW.

Doing nothing sounds easy. But many of us feel pressure to always keep busy, so we don't often allow ourselves the luxury of doing nothing.

Find a comfortable spot where you can sit in front of a window with a good view. Set a timer for at least ten minutes.

THEN, SIMPLY LOOK OUT THE WINDOW.

DO:

+ Watch cars or people pass by.
+ Study buildings, trees, or the sky.
+ Hear the wind pick up and die down.

DON'T:

+ Have a conversation with someone.
+ Send a text, take a photo, or look at a screen.
+ Fall asleep.

This time is for sitting with the wandering contents of your mind and nothing else. Soon, you will get back to the demands of life. But during this set time, press pause.

Allow your quieter, deeper thoughts to rise. Breathe and sit with them.

I CAN
EXAMINE MY
EMOTIONS.

DAY 2

IDENTIFY

IDENTIFYING OUR EMOTIONS IS THE FIRST STEP TO UNDERSTANDING THEM.

Today, when you feel a strong emotion, pause to **simply identify it.**

Do I feel

FRUSTRATED?

Do I feel

ANNOYED OR DEFENSIVE?

Do I feel

EAGER OR EXCITED TO START SOMETHING?

Notice if you can feel the emotion anywhere in your body. **Do you feel it in your shoulders, legs, or chest?**

+ Mime the action of pulling the emotion from your body and placing it on a table in front of you to observe.

+ Then, examine the emotion. What do you think might be causing it? Why do you think this emotion is so strong?

+ When you are done examining your emotion, mime the action of setting it aside on a shelf or in a drawer.

This helps remind you that though the emotion still exists, **it doesn't have to take over your body.**

LIFE IS **CONSTANT** MOTION.

THIS WILL PASS.

DAY 3
LET GO

Worries are a natural part of life. Some are minor: "Am I wearing matching socks?" Others are more serious: "Will I pass today's science test?"

If possible, do this activity while sitting next to a peaceful creek or other stream of water. Otherwise, close your eyes and imagine yourself there.

Picture the sunlight filtering through the trees and speckling the ground below. Hear the sound of leaves rustling, insects humming, and the creek babbling over small rocks. Smell the fresh air and feel its light touch on your skin.

As you watch the water, picture leaves floating atop it and moving along with the current. Imagine each leaf is a troublesome thought related to a worry you've had. As new thoughts bubble up, acknowledge them, then watch them float away.

DO:

+ Allow thoughts to flow through your mind naturally.

+ It's okay if your mind drifts away from your worrying thoughts.

DON'T:

+ Pass any judgment on the thoughts you are experiencing. Regard them the same way you would a leaf floating down a creek.

"EVERYBODY SHOULD BE QUIET NEAR A LITTLE STREAM AND LISTEN."

—Ruth Krauss, *Open House for Butterflies*

21

DAY 4
KNOW YOURSELF

Have you ever thought about what makes *you*? Not your looks, your likes and dislikes, or even how a friend would describe you. But what are the core traits that make up your character?

Make a list of words that describe your character, such as

MORAL, HONEST, EMPATHETIC.

Include some things that might be perceived as negative too, such as

IMPATIENT, SHY, AWKWARD, PICKY.

Now, read your list. Pause at each trait and reflect on it. For the ones that seem negative, ask yourself if there are times when these traits might be helpful to you or others. For the traits you consider positive, think about their possible downsides.

You'll probably find that most traits have more than one side.

THE POINT IS TO TAKE PRIDE IN EVERYTHING THAT MAKES YOU WHO YOU ARE!

BE BOLD. FACE THE POSSIBILITY OF FAILURE.

DAY 5

PRACTICE FAILING

TODAY, TRY DOING SOMETHING YOU'VE TOLD YOURSELF **YOU ARE BAD AT.**

We naturally gravitate toward activities we are good at. But by doing only what we know we're good at, we miss the chance to learn new skills and to practice being bold and flexible.

Choose an everyday activity, such as cooking, singing, playing a sport, or trying to solve a challenging math problem. This should be something you've never thought yourself capable of doing. Take part in this activity

WITHOUT JUDGMENT.

DO:

+ Focus on the physical and mental tasks of the activity.
+ Seek joy in each individual action of the activity.
+ Find a way to make the activity your own.

DON'T:

+ Worry about the end results.
+ Allow your mind to slip into negative self-talk, such as, "I'm bad at this," "I knew I couldn't do it," or "I'll never get it!"

When you're finished, reflect on what you just did. What did you enjoy most about the activity? What surprised you? What was most challenging? What did you notice about the challenging parts? What would you do differently next time? **Allow these thoughts to pass through your mind without judgment.**

"AND NOW THAT YOU DON'T HAVE TO BE PERFECT, YOU CAN BE GOOD."

—John Steinbeck,
East of Eden

DAY 6
NOURISH

When we're busy, we may not take time to savor our food. We scarf down a granola bar on the way to practice or grab a quick bowl of cereal before studying for a test. Too often, we don't put time, thought, and care into the act of eating.

1. Take your time.

2. Spread slowly; cut with care; stir patiently.

3. Set your snack on a table.

THEN SIT DOWN AND EAT.

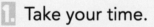

DO:

+ Focus only on the food and experience of eating. Is your food warm or cool? Chewy or crunchy? Sweet or salty? What sounds do you hear when you bite and chew?

DON'T:

+ Multitask while eating, such as working on homework, texting with friends, or reading a book.

When you've finished your snack, notice how you feel, both physically and mentally. **Do you feel energized or sleepy? Rushed or relaxed? Stressed or calm?**

I CAN FIND PEACE

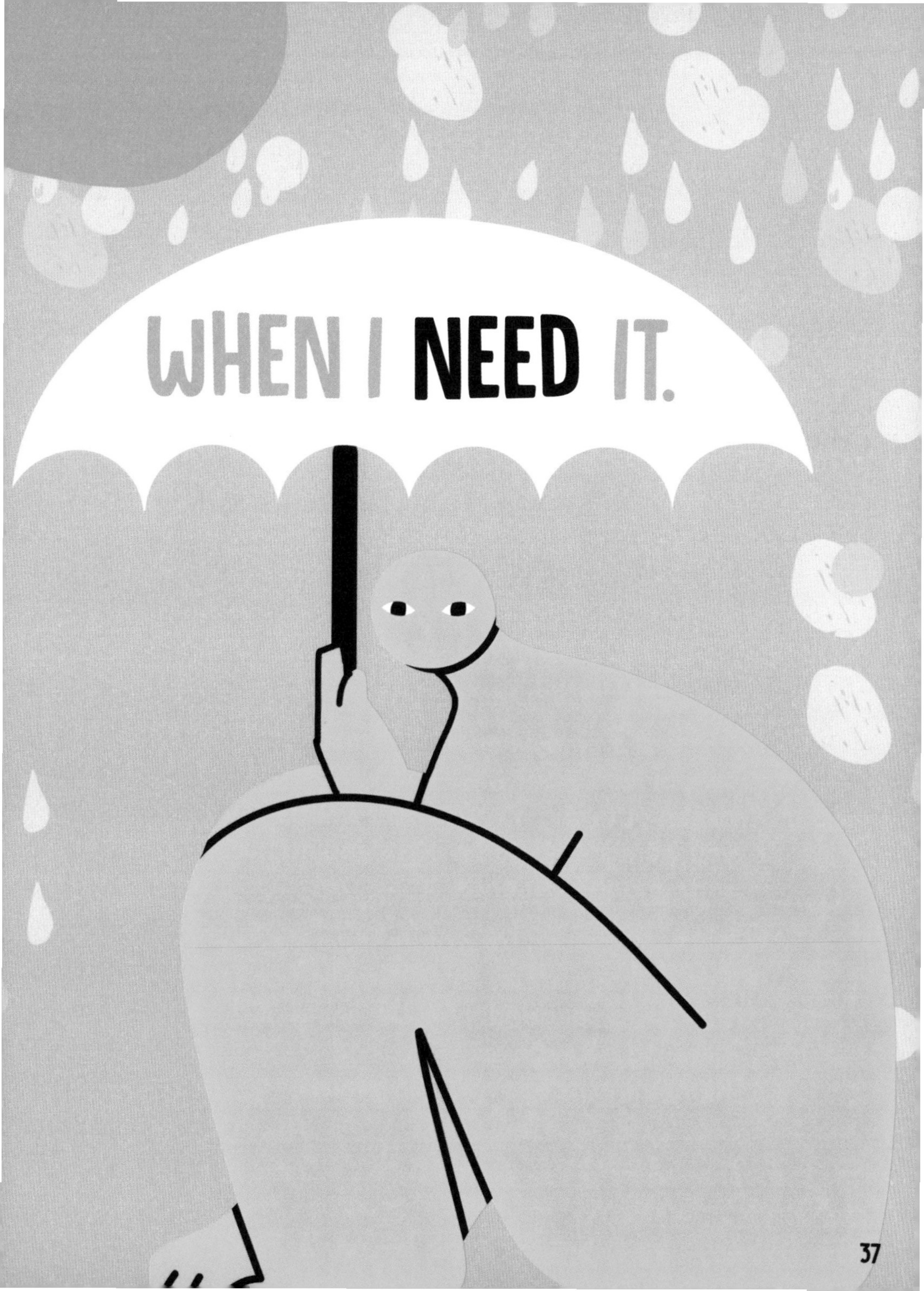
WHEN I NEED IT.

DAY 7
JOURNEY

No matter what is happening around you, you can **choose to feel at peace**—if only for a few minutes.

Sit or lay down in a comfortable position. Set a timer for three minutes. Then close your eyes.

3 min

Think of a time when you felt at peace. Where were you? Maybe you were by the ocean or taking a walk in the woods. Maybe you were snuggled up in a sleeping bag, surrounded by friends.

Allow your mind to explore the memory. Remember the way the air smelled or the waves sounded. Feel the lining of the sleeping bag against your skin. **Remember the feeling of peace.**

When the timer goes off, feel free to stay in your memory longer. When you're ready to reenter the real world, take it slow. Gently wiggle your fingers and toes. Breathe in and breathe out. Take one last thought of your memory before opening your eyes.

ALLOW THIS MEMORY TO BE YOUR INNER PEACE PLACE.

You can return there anytime you want to!

I AM
CAPABLE.

I AM OK.

41

DAY 8

BELIEVE IN YOURSELF

TODAY, REMIND YOURSELF THAT YOU ARE ABLE TO MEET ANY CHALLENGES THAT COME YOUR WAY.

We often associate confident people with taking charge and giving orders. But really, confidence is a **belief in your own self and abilities.**

Today, anytime you face a stressful or challenging situation, remind yourself,

I AM CAPABLE.

I AM OK.

Let these words keep you from spiraling into anxiety. Know that as a human being, you are a natural problem-solver.

YOU HAVE THE SKILLS TO HANDLE WHATEVER THE WORLD THROWS AT YOU.

This does not mean everything will go perfectly for you. That's not how it works for anyone. But your gifts and skills will serve you, no matter what comes your way.

I CAN'T MESS UP AT BEING ME.

DAY 9
OWN WHO YOU ARE

TODAY, EMBRACE WHATEVER IT IS YOU'RE FEELING SELF-CONSCIOUS ABOUT.

It is normal to feel self-conscious. But if that feeling is stopping you from trying new things and being your true self, it's time to send it packing.

MAYBE it's your newfound interest in playing the bassoon or doing origami.

MAYBE it's the funky new sunglasses you bought or the bold new hairstyle you've wanted to try. Or

MAYBE it's those dance moves you've been hiding from your friends.

WHATEVER IT IS,
DO IT, WEAR IT,
AND TOTALLY
OWN IT WITHOUT
FEELING THE
NEED TO EXPLAIN
YOURSELF.

THIS MOMENT IS
FOR ME.

DAY 10
ENJOY

With a steady stream of texts and posts and updates, it's hard to ever feel fully alone with ourselves— **unless we make the time.**

Spend this time doing an activity you enjoy.

Maybe you'll watch a movie or have a picnic lunch in the backyard. Maybe you'll complete a puzzle or walk your dog.

Whatever activity you choose, **do it on your own**—not just physically, but mentally too. Avoid documenting your experience through photos, texts, or posts.

JUST FOCUS ON ENJOYING THE MOMENT FOR YOURSELF.

WHEN WE LEARN
TO ENJOY OUR OWN
COMPANY, WE GAIN
A CLEARER SENSE OF
WHO WE ARE
AND OUR PLACE IN
THE WORLD.

BREATHE

Life can be overwhelming, whether things are good or bad, chaotic or dull. We have expectations for how we should feel and act, how events should unfold, and what we should accomplish. It's no wonder we often find ourselves feeling stressed, anxious, or rushed.

As our bodies go through the motions of the task at hand, our minds often wander between the past and future. *Why did I say that? Next time I have to do better. If only that hadn't happened. What if I don't get what I want?*

The next ten challenges in this book encourage you to practice presence. This is the skill of fully experiencing the here and now. One way to focus on the moment is through mindful breathing. Setting screens aside helps too. You might even find presence by giving yourself over to the unpredictable flow of life.

When you practice presence, you ground yourself in what is real and true right now. You learn to put your energy into what you can control while accepting the things you can't. This will leave you better equipped to find peace in your surroundings, starting with simply taking a

MOMENT TO BREATHE.

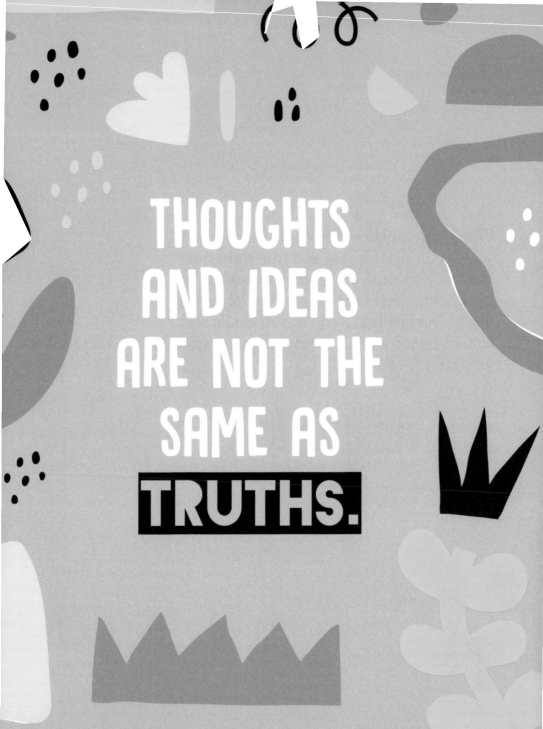

THOUGHTS AND IDEAS ARE NOT THE SAME AS TRUTHS.

FACT CHECK

TODAY, TRAIN YOUR BRAIN TO SEPARATE FACT FROM FICTION.

In just one hour, your brain can have thousands of thoughts. Some are neutral, some are positive, and some are negative. But are these thoughts **true** or **false?**

Write down a list of every negative thought you are conscious of today.

They could be worries, concerns, or just thoughts bringing you down. Some parts of these thoughts may be objective facts. Others are assumptions—you can't verify they are true. For example:

THOUGHT: I am a bad writer. I got a D on my English paper.

THOUGHT: My friends don't like me. They hung out on Friday night without me.

Review your list of thoughts. Think about whether each one is a known fact or an assumption. Maybe part of the thought is a fact and part is an assumption. Circle anything that is an assumption and reflect on it. Assumptions are not always true! Does acknowledging this change the importance you give them?

Go back to your list of thoughts. This time, underline any facts. Now, write down one positive assumption or one positive fact related to each one.

Thought: I am a bad writer. I got a D on my English paper.

POSITIVE FACT: I am a good student. I just didn't study the paper's topic enough.

Thought: My friends don't like me. They hung out on Friday night without me.

POSITIVE ASSUMPTION: There could be many reasons they didn't invite me. Maybe they went to the skate park, which they know I don't enjoy.

I AM HERE,
FULLY.

DAY 12

UNPLUG

We look at screens for schoolwork, TV, messages from friends, and social media updates. Keeping tabs on so many things at once can be overwhelming! **It leaves our days fragmented and our minds overloaded.**

When you're riding in a bus or car, **look out the window instead of at a screen.**

When you're walking the dog or meeting your friends, **keep your phone tucked away.**

When you're sitting down to dinner with your family, **leave your phone, tablet, or portable gaming device behind.**

And if you can't avoid using a screen, **focus on one screen at a time.**

WHEREVER YOU ARE, BE THERE FULLY. PAY ATTENTION TO WHAT IS HAPPENING RIGHT HERE, RIGHT NOW.

You might find that less screen time makes you feel more relaxed, peaceful, and present.

I APPRECIATE LIFE'S SIMPLE MOMENTS.

DAY 13

SAVOR

Anticipating future events is fun, but it can also bring anxiety. That is why it is a good exercise, every now and then, to **limit your plans and expectations to today only.**

Decide what you can manage to make happen today.

It doesn't have to be anything big. In fact, the simpler it is, the better.

Maybe it's a walk in the park or a picnic with a friend.

Maybe it's a bike ride to the neighborhood ice cream shop after dinner.

BY KEEPING YOUR PLANS SIMPLE AND YOUR EXPECTATIONS LIMITED TO TODAY, YOU CAN PRACTICE SAVORING AND BEING GRATEFUL FOR WHAT IS WITHIN YOUR GRASP RIGHT NOW.

I OPEN MYSELF
TO THE
WONDER
AND
WILDNESS
OF THE
UNIVERSE.

DAY 14

EMBRACE CHAOS

So much of life is entirely out of our control. That can be frustrating, unpredictable, and overwhelming. But it can also present **beautiful possibilities**.

Visit two natural spaces. If you can't physically visit them, then travel to them in your mind.

The first is a neat, orderly, well-tended space, such as a rose garden, golf course, or perfectly manicured front yard. How does this space make you feel?

Next, visit a wilder space. It could be a weed-filled corner of your backyard or a park no one ever visits. Or maybe it's a ditch filled with wildflowers. At first glance, it may look like a mess. But observe all the life crammed into this space. Notice the many plants, insects, birds, and other animals. Watch how they grow together and interact. How does this space make you feel?

Reflect on what you experienced. Which space is richer and more interesting? Which has more opportunity for growth and change?

Today, focus on allowing your life to be wild instead of tidy. Remind yourself that complexity and chaos make life richer and more interesting.

THE WILDNESS ALLOWS FOR POSSIBILITIES YOU'D NEVER FIND IN SOMETHING SUPER ORDERLY.

I TAKE TIME TO OBSERVE.

DAY 15
OBSERVE

When we feel stressed or hurried, we can slow down by observing familiar places with **new eyes.**

Go to a room in your home where you spend the most time or feel most at ease.

As you step into the room, **pretend you are a traveler entering a foreign land.**

Gaze at each item, object, and piece of furniture within the room. **Try to look at them with fresh eyes.**

Notice how light hits the walls and fills the room. Listen to the sounds of your steps on the floor. Pick things up and turn them over. **Think about the textures, colors, and smells.**

Take your time and observe with care. When you feel satisfied with your observations, sit down and take a few breaths.

GROUND YOURSELF

IN THIS NEWLY FAMILIAR SPACE.

In 1790, Frenchman Xavier de Maistre was arrested after a duel and imprisoned to his room for six weeks. He filled his time by taking a journey around his room and writing about it. In 1794, his work *Voyage autour de ma chambre*, or *A Journey around My Room*, was published.

"WHEN I TRAVEL IN MY ROOM, I SELDOM KEEP TO A STRAIGHT LINE."

—Xavier de Maistre, *A Journey around My Room* (translated from French)

I FIND PEACE IN SOOTHING SPACES.

DAY 16
SOOTHE

Our environments have lots of influence over our states of mind. What could you do to make your current environment **more soothing?**

Think of the area of your home where you spend the most time, like your bedroom or a reading nook.

How could you transform this space to be more calming or to bring you peace?

You can start by reducing clutter. Then, try adding soft lights, houseplants, or your favorite scents. Consider a few soothing, natural colors for the walls and decor.

(Be sure to get an adult's permission before painting walls, hanging art, or making other big changes!)

DO:

+ Keep items that bring you peace, joy, and happiness.
+ Keep items that serve a practical purpose.
+ Look for creative ways to organize your space.

DON'T:

+ Add more clutter to your space. For any item you add, remove another item.
+ Feel pressure to keep items you associate with negative thoughts or memories, or items you have no use for anymore—even if those items were gifts.
+ Let this project overwhelm you. If redecorating feels daunting, focus on one thing you can do today to make your space more peaceful. It may be as simple as making your bed or putting away clean laundry!

I SEE BEAUTY IN THE ORDINARY.

DAY 17
HONOR THE ORDINARY

TODAY, SEE THE BEAUTY AND HUMANITY IN THE ORDINARY AND IMPERFECT.

We often feel the desire to be extraordinary, impressive, and successful. This can be a big source of anxiety, especially when those around us seem to broadcast perfection.

As you go about your day, take photos or draw sketches of objects or moments that are perfectly ordinary.

Sketch a simple peanut butter and jelly sandwich.

Create a drawing of an afternoon nap.

Snap a photo of the overflowing junk drawer in the kitchen.

AT THE END OF THE DAY, LOOK THROUGH THESE REFLECTIONS OF ORDINARY LIFE.

Take a moment to contemplate what is depicted in each image. Why is it important? What feelings, tasks, or memories are tied to it?

I WON'T STRESS ABOUT STRESS.

DAY 18

ACCEPT

Too much stress and anxiety can be harmful. But worries and stress are a natural part of life. Doing away with them is not always helpful. Sometimes, anxiety can be a good thing! In fact, anxiety probably kept early humans safe. Being anxious about dangerous animals, for example, would have urged these humans to avoid them.

You may not need to worry about encountering an ancient saber-toothed tiger, but anxiety still can play a helpful role in your life. **Anxiety can make you a better leader or a better friend. It can motivate you to do your best.**

Maybe you were worried about a test, so you made an extra effort to study. Maybe you were anxious a friend was upset with you, so you reached out to her, making your friendship stronger.

MAKE A MENTAL LIST OF TIMES YOUR ANXIETY SERVED YOU.

Let it remind you that your worries don't always have to weigh you down. They can have the power to help you make better decisions and prepare you to handle whatever challenges life throws your way!

I CAN **CONTROL** MY BREATH.

DAY 19
BREATHE

When your mind is racing, controlled breathing can help **slow it down**.

This is a breathing exercise you can do just about anywhere, whether you're in class, at home, or out with friends.

First, breathe all the air out of your lungs.

Breathe in through your nose for a count of

4 SECONDS.

Hold your breath for

7 SECONDS.

Then breathe out through your mouth for

8 SECONDS,

pushing the air through your pursed lips to make a "whoosh" sound.

REPEAT THE 4-7-8 CYCLE A FEW TIMES UNTIL YOU FEEL MORE RELAXED.

TODAY IS
A RIVER,
AND I WILL
FLOW
WITH THE
CURRENT.

93

DAY 20
FLOW

A "flow state" means you are totally immersed in an activity to the point that it feels effortless. It's as if the world and any obstacles around you disappear. Some call it being **"in the zone."**

Most of our lives are packed with schedules, routines, and expectations.

Today, allow yourself to set as many of these things aside as possible. Keep any important health-related routines. But

DON'T DECIDE

what the day will include, what you will do, or how it will end.

ALLOW YOURSELF TO FLOW WITH THE CURRENT OF THE DAY.

Embrace unexpected events or challenges. You can practice doing this by adopting the philosophy of an improvisational actor. When something unexpected comes your way, say, "Yes, and . . ." **This means you accept and then react to this unexpected thing in a positive, productive way.**

WU WEI

Daoism is an ancient Chinese philosophy. It teaches its followers to embrace simplicity in life and open themselves up to the *dao*, the "path" or "way."

One fundamental aspect of Daoism is *wu wei*, the concept of "non-doing" or "doing nothing." This does not mean being lazy, but embracing effortless action, such as swimming with—rather than against—the currents. Wu wei encourages giving oneself over to the ups and downs of existence. It urges unity between an individual and the environment, so the two **coexist in harmony.**

BE

So much in life comes down to you: how *you* feel, how *you* cope, how *you* respond to a situation. It's easy to feel like the way your life unfolds falls squarely on your shoulders. But you are not an island! You share this world and this life with others through all kinds of relationships.

These relationships include people who love you, support you, and laugh with you. You also have people in your life who coach you, teach you, and wave to you as they deliver your mail. Some relationships you form may last a lifetime. Others will be short interactions, maybe lasting only minutes. And even people you never meet may, in some indirect way, affect or be affected by you. All these people make life more interesting, colorful, and rich. And *you* provide these things to others! Others need you, and you need them too.

CHALLENGES 20–30

The final ten challenges of this book ask you to reflect on and grow in the way you relate to others. These challenges will push you to be honest, to be sorry, and to be trusting. You'll practice being there for others, being compassionate, and being a force of good in the world.

YOU'LL PRACTICE BEING.

I LISTEN WITH MY **HEART,** **SOUL,** AND **MIND.**

DAY 21
LISTEN

When a friend shares a problem with us, our automatic response might be to try to find the bright side. But often what a person in pain needs is for someone else to simply **acknowledge** and **understand** what they are feeling.

Begin by asking a friend a specific question about something you know is going on in their life. ("How are you?" doesn't count!)

REALLY LISTEN TO THE ANSWER.

Observe your friend's body language to see if that gives you clues to how they are feeling. Then ask follow-up questions. Put yourself in their shoes and try to imagine how you would feel if you were in a similar circumstance. Understand that everybody reacts to situations differently.

DO:

+ Focus on the person and acknowledge what they are feeling.

+ Let them know you understand why they feel the way they do, and that it is OK for them to feel that way.

+ Follow their lead. Don't push them to express emotions or share details if they aren't comfortable doing so.

+ Reassure them you are there for them no matter what. They aren't alone.

DON'T:

+ Judge their feelings or second-guess whether those feelings are valid.

+ Try to change the subject out of discomfort.

+ Respond with, "At least . . ."

+ Offer advice (unless they specifically ask for it).

Know you may not be able to help beyond listening and understanding. Remember, this is not about you. **You are giving the gift of empathy to someone in need.**

"WHEN YOU TALK, YOU ARE ONLY REPEATING WHAT YOU ALREADY KNOW. BUT IF YOU LISTEN, YOU MAY LEARN SOMETHING NEW."

—Dalai Lama

I AM OPEN AND HONEST.

DAY 22
SPEAK

When you're upset with someone, you have **two options:** You can grow moodily silent and turn your back, or you can say something.

If you disagree with someone,

RESPECTFULLY EXPLAIN WHY TO THEM.

If someone says something that hurts you,

TELL THEM HOW YOU FEEL.

If someone is bothering you, politely but firmly

ASK THEM TO STOP.

DO:

+ Explain your feelings with patience and compassion.

DON'T:

+ Assume the other person knows why you are upset.

Speaking openly and honestly can be a great relief from the burden of holding a grudge.

I AM NOT MY MISTAKES.

DAY 23
REPAIR

We're often hard on ourselves when we make mistakes. But mistakes are a part of life! Take responsibility, make things right, and forgive yourself.

Everyone has faults, and we all make mistakes every day.

Some are minor—we spilled some milk or forgot to change the laundry. Other mistakes are larger—we snapped at a friend and hurt their feelings, we broke a sibling's favorite possession, or we dented a parent's car.

It can be tempting to make excuses for these mistakes, or even pretend they never happened. Other times, we let guilt and shame about these errors consume us.

Make a point today to acknowledge, accept, and own your mistakes—big or small.

If you owe someone an apology, offer it freely, with no conditions, excuses, or expectations of instant forgiveness. Then forgive yourself too. Give yourself some grace. **Accept that you made a mistake and move on.**

YOUR FAULTS OR ERRORS DO NOT DEFINE WHO YOU ARE.

I SEE AND ACKNOWLEDGE THE LIVES AROUND ME.

CONNECT

TODAY, CONNECT WITH THE PEOPLE YOU PASS.

Making eye contact sounds simple enough. But for many of us, it feels more natural to look away.

Whether you're walking the dog, on your way to class, or running errands with a parent, practice looking up and out.

See the people who go to your school and live in your neighborhood, and acknowledge their presence with eye contact.

You'll likely feel a natural urge to look down or away. **Actively work against this urge.**

Not everyone will meet your eyes, and that is okay. Don't think of it as rejection. Instead, remind yourself that others may have a hard time making eye contact too.

When you do catch someone's eye, give a small nod or smile of acknowledgment.

NOTICE HOW GOOD IT FEELS TO SEE AND BE SEEN BY ANOTHER.

Know that others feel just as good about seeing and being seen by you.

I AM
NOT
ALONE.

DAY 25
ASK

We often keep our guards up. Maybe we think this gives others the impression we're strong and capable. Or maybe we feel uncomfortable being vulnerable. But this isolates us from the people who care about us.

Vulnerability means putting yourself in a place where you could be emotionally hurt or let down. It is important to practice being vulnerable with people you feel safe with. But even then, allowing yourself to be vulnerable can be scary. It means shedding the armor you wear and putting yourself at the mercy of others.

Exposing our vulnerabilities brings us closer to others, however. It makes us more relatable. It also gives others the opportunity to share their vulnerabilities with us, and it opens lines of communication.

So, ask for help with homework or a chore. Share something that has been troubling you. Allow yourself to express an emotion you've been trying to hide from the rest of the world.

YOU MAY BE
SURPRISED HOW GOOD
YOU FEEL AFTER
ALLOWING PEOPLE
YOU TRUST TO
SEE THESE
PARTS OF YOU.

I REGARD
OTHERS WITH
GENEROSITY AND
COMPASSION.

DAY 26

BE GENEROUS

"He is such a slob." "She is so weird." "What were they thinking?" "What are they wearing?"

Words of judgment tend to roll off our tongues with little to no thought. But other people deserve the same grace we give ourselves.

Every time you're about to make a statement about another person, ask yourself:

+ Is what I'm about to say even slightly negative?

+ Am I passing judgment on something this person cannot control?

+ Am I passing judgment on a form of self-expression that is harmless to others?

+ Am I passing judgment on a mistake this person made?

If the answer to any of these questions is yes, try to be generous. Imagine what it feels like to be judged for something you cannot control. Imagine what it feels like to be judged for the way you choose to express yourself. Imagine what might lead someone to behave in a certain way.

Be gracious with your assumptions. Acknowledge that you are just as prone to making mistakes as other people are.

YOU MIGHT FIND THAT BEING KIND AND GENEROUS TO OTHERS MAKES YOU FEEL BETTER ABOUT YOURSELF.

I HELP
MYSELF
BY HELPING
OTHERS.

127

DAY 27
HELP

Sometimes we get caught up in our own troubles.
One way to feel better is by looking outside ourselves and asking what we can do for others.

Science has shown that giving back to others is an excellent way to improve your own mental health.

Today, look for the people around you who may be struggling—in both big and small ways. Think about little things you can do to help them.

+ Maybe there is a new kid in town who always sits alone at lunch. Offer to sit with them and ask how they're adjusting—and really listen to their answer.

+ Maybe your mom seems stressed after work. Tell her you will make dinner and clean up afterward.

+ Offer to tutor a classmate you know is struggling in a class you're doing well in.

+ Take a walk and collect every bit of trash you pass.

+ Find ways you can volunteer in your community.

NOTICE HOW IT FEELS TO FOCUS ON THE NEEDS OF OTHERS FOR A WHILE.

Does it feel good to take the focus off yourself? Do your own troubles carry less weight?

I CHOOSE JOY, NOT JEALOUSY.

DAY 28
BE GRATEFUL

Envy can strain relationships. But we all have that friend—the one who seems to have it all. We can't help but think, "My life would be better if it were more like theirs."

Think about a person you know and have envied.

Write down all the things they have that you'd like to have. This could be their good looks, musical talent, or athletic ability. Maybe it's their boyfriend or girlfriend, their swimming pool, or their drum set.

Now, make a list of all the things *you* have and feel lucky for. Include things big and small, and both physical and intangible, such as things related to your passions, talents, interests, and relationships.

The point of these lists isn't to compare and decide who is most fortunate.

IT IS TO UNDERSTAND THAT EVERYONE IS LUCKY IN SOME WAYS AND LACKING IN OTHERS.

After you've listed everything you feel lucky to have, revisit the list you made for the person you envy. As you reread the list, allow yourself to feel happy for that person instead. You will likely find that rather than feeling envious and negative, you will feel **grateful** and **positive!**

I EXPRESS MY GRATITUDE.

DAY 29
THANK

TODAY, GO OUT OF YOUR WAY TO SHARE YOUR GRATITUDE AND APPRECIATION.

Identifying what you're grateful for feels good. Thanking those you're grateful for **feels even better.**

Think of everyone who contributes to your well-being.

These are the people who listen to you, teach you, serve you lunch, coach your sports teams, make you dinner, and drive you to school.

They're also the ones who bring you joy and keep you company, such as your friends and family members.

Now, share your appreciation for these people! You can do this with a smile, a thank-you, a note, or a phone call. Even the smallest gestures of gratitude can have a huge impact.

HOW DOES IT FEEL TO LET SOMEONE KNOW THEY'RE IMPORTANT TO YOU?

MY WAY.

DAY 30
TRUST

Feelings of doubt, suspicion, and uncertainty wear us down. The cure for that? **A healthy dose of trust.**

 that there are people in your life who believe in you.

 that your friends care about you.

 that you can handle any challenges that arise.

 that uncertainties will resolve in time.

TRUST THAT
YOU WILL
LEARN AS YOU
GROW AND
EXPERIENCE
LIFE.

"BE PATIENT TOWARD ALL THAT IS UNSOLVED IN YOUR HEART AND TRY TO LOVE THE QUESTIONS THEMSELVES, LIKE LOCKED ROOMS AND LIKE BOOKS THAT ARE NOW WRITTEN IN A VERY FOREIGN TONGUE. DO NOT NOW SEEK THE ANSWERS, WHICH CANNOT BE GIVEN YOU BECAUSE YOU WOULD NOT BE ABLE TO LIVE THEM. AND THE POINT IS TO LIVE EVERYTHING. LIVE THE QUESTIONS NOW. PERHAPS YOU WILL THEN GRADUALLY, WITHOUT NOTICING IT, LIVE ALONG SOME DISTANT DAY INTO THE ANSWER."

—Rainer Maria Rilke,
Letters to a Young Poet

CONCLUSION

Reflect, Accept, and Grow

Japanese culture honors the ancient practice of *kintsugi*. This is the art of repairing broken pottery using liquid gold or silver. The resulting metallic veins highlight the journey of the object, cracks and all. The philosophy behind kintsugi applies to more than just pottery. It celebrates the imperfections that make an individual not only more beautiful, but entirely unique.

Consider this philosophy as you reflect on your thirty-day journey to peace and presence. What have you learned about yourself? What has changed about the way you engage with your emotions and the world around you? Try to accept and even celebrate all the parts of you that are imperfect or in progress. Embrace the scars you carry. Let them enhance the beautiful and unique person you are and will continue to become.

Allow the challenges in this book to continue to push, encourage, and support you. Revisit the mantras that resonated with you and let them guide more growth. With whatever life throws your way, always remember to

PAUSE,
BREATHE,
AND BE.